the seven wonders of stevie

the seven wonders of stevie

Kwansabas

Ran Walker

BLACK + SQUARE PAPERBACK EDITION

© 2026 Randolph Walker, Jr.

Cover Photo Courtesy of Motown Records (Public Domain)
Cover Design by Randolph Walker, Jr.
AI Cartoon Image of Stevie Wonder Against Seven Wonders

"Writing About Love" was previously published in *50-Word Stories*.

ISBN: 978-1-961753-20-4 (Paperback)
ISBN: 978-1-961753-21-1 (Ebook)

First Edition
10 9 8 7 6 5 4 3 2

Black + Square, LLC
Hampton, VA

contents

part four
the wonder of justice

part five
the wonder of time

part six
the wonder of soul

part seven
the wonder of legacy

For Stevland Hardaway Morris
and
James Walker Bishop

preface

When Dr. Eugene Redmond created the kwansaba, I would become only one of many who embraced this poetic form and published collections of them. In fact, I wrote my first collection of kwansabas, *Most of My Heroes Don't Appear On No Stamps* (University of Hell Press, 2019), and was pleasantly surprised at how well it was received.

A kwansaba is a form of poetry that is built off of sevens: seven lines, seven words per line, and no word of more than seven letters (excluding foreign words and proper nouns). Even more, the form is about the celebration of African-American culture.

When I look back over the first 50 years of my life, Stevie Wonder's music has always been there. Even in several of my earlier books, I referenced his music as a way of signaling to the reader the overall vibe I was going for. When I decided to write another collection of kwansabas, I knew I wanted to make Stevie the focus of the book.

The title of this book came about serendipitously, though. The phrase "Seven Wonders of the World" is ingrained in our cultural lexicon to reference magnificent locations that defy our greatest expectations, and if I were to look at the seven wonders of contemporary music, Stevie Wonder would be an indisputable wonder, as he is one of the greatest musical geniuses of our times. It just so happens that his stage name is "Wonder," which is more than apt. The seven part also speaks to the foundation of the kwansaba form.

I considered doing a collection of strictly biographical poems as many amazing poets have done for other celebrated individuals, but there is more than enough already written about how Stevie Wonder was a precocious musical prodigy signed to Motown at the age of 11 and how he had a magnificent run of classic albums throughout the 70s, groove-filled soundtracks of the 80s and 90s, and outstanding political activism that helped MLK Day to come into existence. This collection, however, is inspired by Stevie Wonder, not exactly a biography of him.

If you would like to do a more biographical deep-dive into Stevie Wonder, I encourage you to listen to the podcast "The Wonder of Stevie" (not related to this book) by Pulitzer-Prize winning cultural critic Wesley Morris, which is available on all major podcasting platforms.

I hope you enjoy my exploration of Stevie Wonder over these seven sections of seven kwansabas each, and hopefully you will grow to appreciate this legend as much as I do.

—Ran Walker, 2025

Music, at its essence, is what gives us memories.

Stevie Wonder

part one
the wonder of sound

pots and pans

mama say don't beat the pots and
pans, my kitchen ain't no club, boy,
but he can't stop the rhythm flowin,
the music comin through finger snaps and
snare pops, and he knows mama will
play that beat on his rump like
max roach, kickin ass and takin names

eleven

when i was eleven, i was dancing
to michael jackson, white glove and all,
hiding action figures deep in my pockets,
began to notice that girls were cute,
and nowhere in this mix was i
blazing with talent in such a way
that i could ever sign with motown

bigger than him

i heard stevie blowing that big harp,
sound rising higher than he could stand,
notes soaring softly through hot summer air,
i stopped to catch each bold breath,
he pulled soul out of the sky,
each note a prayer shaped by wind,
small boy lost in sound so big

detroit

we build autos here and even tunes
but not auto tunes cause the corp
only plays for those who could be
legends guiding future artists like aged maps
tracing wide detroit streets with every route,
even to memphis stacks, where our cars
bump like shaft on their green tvs

jammin on the one

In memory of mjw

we all wanted to be like theo
and denise, struck by the world of
stevie, our voices tamed by his fingers,
a part of a song being written
and shared with us to share with
others so they would know we too
could be a part of black genius

# of gods and griots

she is lost in an a flat
7, a cloud like 9 that takes
her, as a soft kiss sewed into
the sun's garden, he plays for her
a spell cast from ivory and strings,
and she inhales this musical aroma of
gods and griots and sparks her soul

genius

it is too easy to call someone
genius and ignore nuance and why it
is so or how it makes you
feel or makes you breathe or makes
you love all that is around you,
genius like oxygen in the air held
in our chests until we fill up

part two
the wonder of vision

memory

you are a memory of the moment
i allowed myself to believe in love
again and forget pain once slapped me
silly, bruises on my heart from beating
too hard against my rib cage, hoping
for more than you could give, than
a soul like me could ever deserve

pranking

celebs say that stevie can see, even
pranks them with *let me drive today*
and *let's video chat* and all manner
of antics he finds funny, and while
they laugh along, they do so not
sure if this is really a prank
and stevie has been faking all along

my mind's eye

for elle

i see us holding hands in the
park, your smile lit by the glow
of the moon, our first kiss moments
away, words heavy on my tongue, eager
to say these three words, to be
the last to say them to you
and hear them said back to me

i dream of colors

at night i dream of colors i
cannot name, shades and hues between night
and day, a melodic chain dancing across
the sky, i want to name them,
one by one, but they are better
felt as one would the rhythm of
a ribbon flowing through stevie's grand piano

planted

she does not believe in naïve ideas
of utopia, but she sees a chance
for love to heal wounds, bind broken
bones, be a salve for pain from
history and failure, face lifted to open
sky, where clouds cry and earth eases
up through cracks to reveal her future

hero

black man super hero, no crush on
wanda, only wonder, this music taking flight,
this vision of power shakes earth and
snaps fingers like thanos, turns dust to
dreams, sound tracks foot steps, soft like
angel kisses that rest above lashes, tasting
sunset where orbs ascend into black night

shallow

ray holding wrists as if waists can't
be held or soft lips enjoyed, voices
like music, laughs and hums calling out
to me like soulful sirens, now that
i have trained my heart to see
beyond the shallow waters that once held
me like a lost little black boy

part three
the wonder of love

she is lovely

for zoë

it's not an inquiry, it's a fact
my little girl's smile can push clouds
away like cotton candy melting on eager
tongues, make storm showers turn to drips,
this smile, the best part of me,
lovely as lovely can be, makes my
grown heart frolic like black boy joy

sending one his love

he will send her a flower, glowing
like stars across a distant galaxy, and
she will hold this flower's secret life
against her bosom and accept this act
of love, watered by synths and strings
that dangle from heart shaped kites kissed
by the lips of the most high

phoenix

she twirls above the wind grate, red
dress flowing in the breeze, gams like
venus, hips like saturn, my eyes drink
this elixir and i am drunk with
fire and if she were to look
at me i would burn up and
like a phoenix i'd be born again

i can't help it

i can't help how i feel when
the music signals your entry into this
room nor would i want to change
a thing about what stirs within, brewing
like kenyan beans slow roasted with care,
you are the magic in my mood
my shelter, my sanctum, my lyric unsung

always

i will love you beyond all the
spheres in the heavens, eternal like natural
numbers or the depth of a black
hole, you fill me up, a rocket
taking flight, and when all is reduced
to dust my love for you will
remain like ancient ruins from beyond time

angel

love is a little black girl with
wings and halo, though her wings don't
always fly and her halo can cock
itself slant like cursive or classic rhymes
because love is not perfect, only patient
and kind, her tender soles walking through
open hearts like dr. daniel hale williams

love songs

love songs should be poems, not 90s
remixes where booty is the only booty
pirates seek, but critics will argue marvin
giving head is worse and stevie out
of touch, but what was good in
the 70s is good for his 70s
and the song is eternal like love

part four
the wonder of justice

destination: brightest star

freedom, seven letters, a state of mind,
a spacial reality, a gift from Jah,
what some people steal for and others
die for, a respect for life and
how it is lived, no master we
blast them and jam on, feeling free
in our skins, in our aching souls

january

let's crown the third monday of the
year, so that we'd be kings for
a day, peace in our dreams of
life, united like fingers of a fist,
shared history shared without picking sides or
making someone the *other*, we are we
and freedom rings like angelic bells tolling

children

to see the world through stevie's eyes
is to see the good in people,
to see them all as boys and
girls, kids with hearts bigger than their
sizes, people worthy of love and respect,
people who deserve to be free of
harm and the evils of the world

privilege

they look down from the top floor
and see the people in the alley
looking for food, warmth, a place to
sleep, and *they* take out their phones,
make videos, post words, *like* this or
that and make *them* of them, a
tale of caution about failing at life

living for the city

one foot off the bus and the
city drinks me like a shot of
joe, store brand, nothing fancy, no sugar,
no cream, just melted dreams that pass
through bowels and on into the gutter
and they call all of this *living*,
if you're from a place under ground

if you really wanna hear our view

he ain't foolin no one, cause he
ain't never known nothin, cared to know
nothin bout us, only bout money, power
gettin cozy with the elite, turnin tricks
to the highest bidder, letting his shit
trickle down on us, his tricky ass,
we are not amused by this clown

bury me in ghana

when i die, bury me in ghana,
my remains finally free on native soil,
let my family rejoice that i am
home, let detroit mourn its musical son,
a life in the key of love,
and take with it the lesson of
charity for the unseen, unheard, and unloved

part five

the wonder of time

time waits for no man

i move through time kissing the future
like we are at the end of
our first date, and i look at
her and say *what next* and she
says *I already know but I won't
spoil it for you*, so I wait
for time to bring me to her

contusion

another word for bruise, like the one
on stevie's brain, crashed car, almost left
us like kids in carts at the
food mart, but he stayed behind, pushed
his life force through black and white
keys, greg* helping round out the dream
showing how his music desires to survive

---

* Greg Phillinganes, famed pianist and arranger, who worked with
Quincy, MJ, Anita, and Stevie. He plays the more challenging key-
board parts on the song "Contusion."

timeless

she is now big enough to ride
shotgun and pick the songs from my
phone to play as i drive her
to school and she settles on a
song from before even I was born
and as she sings along with stevie
i realize that his songs defy time

.

chasing seasons

she told me she loved me in
fall so i fell in love with
her and fell into winter where she
left me cold and alone, but i
tried to find my way back into
her life in spring but all i
had was a summer that never was

magic and love

stevie said magic should be eternal, that
love should be *always* like when day
becomes the night and night becomes the
day, and if both these things were
to last forever, we'd have to admit
love is magic and magic is love,
and neither of them will ever end

hip hop in space

break boys groove to loops of "all
day sucker" while djs watch purple lines
and keep the party jumping like popcorn
in pots, waved over gas stoves, night
finding us glowing beneath street lamps like
a group of stars from the deepest
black of space, where there's no sound

writing about love

my notepad is full of poems about
love back from a time i didn't
know much about it, though i thought
i did, but love must be learned
by living through its highs and lows,
my notepad growing as i grew to
find myself this man writing about love

part six

the wonder of soul

motor city

he is tempted to lounge around the
studio, listen to singers sing—supreme voices
top charts but start here first, motor
city soul, while fingers snap, catchy cadence
and like a sponge, he absorbs each
note, melody, voice, breath, writing in a
quiet corner, waiting until it's his turn

sanctuary

my catalog is a bible unto itself,
singers chant verses, hum hymns penned in
my studio, finding food, bread but not
crumbs, filling their bellies with my music
taking this love to more people, virus
of agape from which we never heal,
singing a life of song as one

black boy in space

black boy in space, night star aglow,
you are safe in dreams of rhythms
of strings, toms, horns, keys, and guitars,
music your armor, your oxygen, while you
venture through space, passing planets like
     peonies
in a field where secret lives abound,
rich fruit, divine sweet nectar of euterpe

boy wonder

james and aretha flow through his veins,
ray, jackie, duke, marvin, and sam, all
vitamin soul, sunrays feeding the seed until
it sprouts from the earth, its roots
deep, its height no ceiling, grazing heaven,
making angels dance—*get down*—at the
great boy wonder who has now arrived

rocket love

ooh, stevie said you dropped his black
ass back down to this cold, cold
world—now why you wanna do that—
but muses be like that some time,
one moment a work of art, the
next she's dumped you like a bad
habit, rocket leaving behind only this song

saturday afternoon

sitting on the couch, album cover on
my lap, trying to keep up with
stevie on "do i do," tongue twisted
with sweets, dizzy soloing, while earl and
dennis play, and stevie tries to rap
but gives up and lets the song
devolve into the bare bones of groove

growling

my little sister laughs when stevie does
fozzie bear, making his voice growl, full
of soul, her lilt trying to do
the same, but saying her voice hurts,
itches, burns trying to do "as"or
"living for the city" or any groove
stevie aims to hammer home his message

part seven

the wonder of legacy

on meeting stevie

i met you when i was 16,
fresh off a plane from south korea,
aimless in lax—and there you were,
i ran up to you, shook your
hand, tried to catch your magic in
palm and take it home with me,
an elixir to inspire my own art

human history

if aliens ever came down to earth
and combed the history of humans, i
pray they find your music and listen
to your love and hope for all,
that this would connect to their beings
and let them know that we never
stopped trying to be our better selves

joyful hope

i still wake up and miss michael,
prince, whitney, luther, frankie, marvin, minnie,
    donny,
and so many who shared their talents,
love, and pain with us through mics
and quiet booths, and my heart weeps,
but then I think of you and
my heart smiles with a joyful hope

weddings

when I was much younger, i was
asked to play "ribbon in the sky"
at every other wedding i went to,
so much so that when i met
my special one, we chose not to
use it, as the song was already
infused into the dna of our love

jimbrunski

i can't listen to "sir duke" or
"that girl" without seeing you at the
piano, playing, rocking, feeling music in ways
i envied, grooves without white gloves, pure
art, like fish tanks of notes, where
our hearts were nets careful not to
let a single melodic minnow slip through

2050

in 2050 a person will sit at
a piano and play a song, a
piece of your legacy, and the oldest
of us will smile and find our
voices giving rise to your spirit, united
beneath the banner of your art, and
the song will live on and on

the wonder of the world

they say there are seven of them,
though the meaning changes with time, still
there is only one you, one wonder,
one stevie, so this poem is for
the wonder bigger than pyramid or petra
or taj mahal or even the great
wall of china, it is for you

acknowledgments

First, I'd like to thank my wife and daughter for their endless love and support. I'd also like to thank my family, friends, and fellow creatives.

I also want to thank James Walker Bishop, my cousin and "big brother," for introducing me to Stevie Wonder.

Finally, I want to thank Stevie for giving me a soundtrack for my life.

about the author

Ran Walker (he/him) is the author of over 40 books. His short stories, flash fiction, microfiction, and poetry have appeared in a variety of anthologies and journals.

He is the winner of the Indie Author Project's National Indie Author of the Year Award, the Black Caucus of the American Library Association Best Fiction Ebook Award, the Virginia Indie Author Project Award for Adult Fiction, and the Blind Corner Afrofuturism Microfiction Contest. Ran is an Associate Professor of English and Creative Writing at Hampton University and teaches with Writer's Digest University. He lives in Virginia with his wife and daughter.

also by ran walker

www.ingramcontent.com/pod-product-compliance
Lightning Source LLC
Chambersburg PA
CBHW051228120626
46547CB00013B/1563